Inward

KeiAudra Wright

BookLeaf Publishing

Presentation by *BookLeaf Publishing*

Web: www.bookleafpub.com

E-mail: info@bookleafpub.com

ISBN: 9789357448161

First edition 2022

DEDICATION

Dedicated to the 7-year-old who fell in love with writing and finally was able to realize her dreams.

ACKNOWLEDGEMENT

Much appreciation to my mother for all of her love and support. I know she is smiling down with much pride.

And I am ever so grateful to the BookLeaf crew for their support and hard work.

The Edge

Testing my faith and fate.
As I stand toes clinging to the very corner of the 90-degree cliff.
Finally pushed to the edge.
Tears have been cried.
Blood has been bled.
Anticipating impact.
I think back.
How could I have allowed myself to get this far.
I assumed I was in control.
But once again my heart was ajar.
For another being who was in need of a genuine soul.
I fold
Myself into tiny pieces.
Tucking me away in my pocket.
Until I can find time for releasing.
Like a broken-winged bird nursed back to health.
I sacrifice myself to make sure someone else's boat remains afloat or can be recovered.
But everyone knows burying burdens is not a good practice.
This time will be the last time.
From this point forward I'm choosing me.

Grow

Narrow-mindedness stunts your growth.
Capping your intellectual potential will lead to a life of sameness.
You were birthed to be different.
Accept it.
Reach farther.
Go further.
Move constantly.
You have space to fill.

Being

Experience is the building block of wisdom.
Without it, one only merely exists.

Let's Be Honest

Life will forever be about taking the good with the bad.
Instant gratification rules the pathway to what is desired nowadays.
The journey is taken for granted.
As much as we'd like to be happy on a consistent basis.
It's not realistic.
No one seems to cherish the values and the only focus is materialistic.
Running through people like an Olympian.
It's really sad.
The mate you were looking for, you probably already had.
Your sociopathic ways and egotism got in the way.
Thought the grass was greener on the other side but it still dies when the seasons change.
Emasculating men.
Disrespecting women.
Really on a pathway to a lonely ass ending.
Using upbringings as excuses.
That won't fly too long.
Once you knew better you should've done better to right your wrongs.

Still blaming others for your downfalls.
It's the same old song.
Getting surgery to fill insecure and low self-esteem voids.
Let someone mention counseling though that's a topic you try to avoid.
Buying high priced chains, cars, and clothes.
But the amount you owe in child support only your baby mama knows.
Unsatisfied with many facets of your life.
Having no idea what being an adult is truly like.
Hiding behind pics, likes, and followers.
But on the other side you find that you're really the one following.
Challenge this, and challenge that.
The real challenge is being you no matter the clapback.
So, all I'm saying is falling off and having flaws is inevitable.
That reality in itself doesn't make you ineligible.
And if I offended, it wasn't my intention. I was just stating my perspective.
But life will forever be about taking the good with the bad.

Kink

Spent from losing myself to deem you uncut.
My soul is taking a vow of celibacy.
Weary from your spirit's phallus and the
unmerciful copulation to my essence.
My body is keeping the score.
Kindness misinterpreted.
Accountability has birthed.
Mirrors no longer reflect an image I care for.
Better for it I will be.

Ditty

Reminiscing of good times always bring to mind
good music.
I use it for tranquility.
In hopes of feeding the inner me.
The sound that brings humility that brings the
back of my mind forward.
And when you listen closer you can hear the
soul.
All souls have a theme song.
A dream song.
A “so it seems” song.
“I see the twinkle in your eye” gleam song.
“Make me think about who’s really on my team”
song.
You tell me if I’m wrong.
Enjoying the music that reminds me of poetry
And when combined with the perfect melody
arises the joy and simplicity of memories,
Which transforms it into a defining cry of what
you’re battling in your realm.
An array of emotions and uncontrollable
thoughts.
The songs we listen to on the way to work that
makes us feel like we've paid the cost.

And the lyrics we enjoy when all we can feel is lost.

Falling Apart

Jigsaw puzzles ain't got shit on me.
The difference is no one has invested in
reassembling my pieces into its original portrait.
Hell, my own reflection half the time is a
mystery.
Coming unglued has become too commonplace
for my spirit.
Trying to figure out how to exempt myself from
such a dilemma.
Fighting for a redo to the undoing of me.
See, growing up we're taught to empathize and
relate.
It's not taught in depth how to bring back
together what has been pulled apart.
Falling for the enemies in a friend's disguise.
And at night when I close my eyes
I feel another piece of me come undone.
Although the answer is probably staring me right
in the face.
I fail to recognize it for what it is.
It's hard to see the remedy and recognize its
authenticity.
Experience and influence are the essence of
what shapes advice.
I just hope I come out symmetrical.

Uncovering more pieces and finding some disfigured, and some seemingly unmatching.
Someone seemed to have left some of their own in the process of detaching.
So, if my words seem a bit dark.
Bear with me.
Life can be unkind.
I'm doing the best I can with the cards I've been dealt.
Don't charge it to my heart, charge it to my mind, if I just so happen to not seem to be much help.

Live

Regrets will rear themselves as a reminder to not
take for granted an opportunity.
They exist so one understands the significance
of seizing the moment.
Go with instinct instead of fear.

What We Do To Ourselves

Sometimes we force society's norms onto ourselves.
Everyone is not meant for everything.

Everyone

We all have fallen while merely trying to stand.

Covet

I don't ask for much.
Just a good laugh every day.
I want to be successful, drink incredible wine,
and a consistent desire to slay.
For all my family and friends to achieve their
wildest dreams.
To sleep every night peacefully, and, if any, only
blissful dreams.
I want my damaged relationships mended, and
all my bonds nursed to be unbreakable.
I want to water my life and blossom like a
garden of the world's most precious delectables.

Before

Yester decade was different than what today
seems to be.
Yester year was mighty diverse.
And it seems the me you see today.
Is the yester me you still think I am.

Counterpart

Determined, poised, conversational, intellect.
Longing for the one I can relentlessly be myself with.
One who can match and complement my attributes.

Meant

Finding your equal can be a tricky thing.
You think you know what you want, but you
really have no clue of "what you want" truly
means.

Who Did I Piss Off

Go through the day to day with struggle after struggle.
Tryna make sense of why even bother to hustle.
Doing right by others without an ulterior motive.
While trudging through life constantly feeling demoted.
Bad days will come and that's not hard to grasp.
But for once will the universe get its foot out of my ass.
Done nothing wrong.
Went over and beyond.
But when I put in my bid, the only response I get is no response.
As if what's being asked is too extravagant to give.
Not asking for millions; just asking to live.
If more is what's wanted, then just say the word.
All the extra micro-struggles, one could've been leading the herd.
All blessed with gifts, no one is an exception to the rest.
The assignment was understood yet this journey keeps getting more complex.
When purpose is revealed, it's a test of the wills.

One can't approach it as if it's another run of the mill.
Feeling real behind on the blessing subscription.
Starting to feel like psychiatry is worth the prescription.
Pop a pill with my meal and feel greater later.
If it fails, it'll just give more fuel to the haters.
Feeling like punishment; like everything touched is destined for destruction.
What's being done wrong; please send some instruction.
Fully aware that good help is hard to find.
And it's nowhere in sight when I'm the one running blind.
May even end up helping the right person with the wrong mind.
Why can't I find yourself in the middle of this lifeline.
Uncomfortable in my skin.
Why can't I seem to get ahead?
Up is where I'm fed.
To pieces I am shred.
Don't know how long this might last but thin ice is what I tread.
Reaping the benefits of nothing but making moves like the little engine that could.
Who did I piss off?
Please tell me.
I wish somebody would.

Consider the Source

When faced with criticism be mindful of where it derives.
Let go of that pride.
Allowing fragility to stunt your growth will only produce a mild replica of the greatness from within.
Some things have no protection from defense.
Face value is where they live.
Don't necessarily assume one is attempting to annihilate dreams or persona.
That negative energy is just as contagious as corona.
Depending on the origin it may actually come from a place of meaning well and compassion.
The intent is not to randomly find souls to assassin.
Humans have an innate instinct to defend themselves.
Whether that be physically or when they feel their character is being assaulted.
No need to put that part of yourself up to collect dust on shelves.
Your psyche is an investment not a loan you can default on.

Criticism does not equal attack.
It's not a conviction on what you lack.
If it can be accepted from corporate bumpkins.
Who could give a damn about one's best interest.
Why be it insufferable from a genuine soul who cares about the steps that you're missing?
One's breakability does not negate facts.
It merely makes transparent the impact.
At some point checking yourself is mandatory.
And the more one fights it, the more I want to know the backstory.
Justification and excuses serve no place in personal growth.
Accountability is honestly the best policy to achieve the most.
Stop being afraid of having flaws, denying is just an admission that you have them.
It's not about your shortcomings, but about the growth spurt after one addresses them.

Freedom

Unshackled by the demands and designated
roles of society.
It's no wonder so many these days suffer from
anxiety.
People in general unable to unregretfully be
one's true self.
Striving for the acceptance of those who would
find another leader if you came face-to-face with
your demise today.
Do not hold back.
Hold your ground.
Being you will manifest the right people to be
around.
Live your best life, run your race, and be you.
Joy and happiness are not interchangeable; this I
know to be true.
A different type of normalcy presents itself
when your mind shifts gears and it's gifted with
the response of 'I don't care.'
Seriously.
There's a freedom that exists that is so
liberating, invigorating, therapeutic.
Drugs are no match, nor can they reproduce it.
Allow excitement to grow within you about
whatever ignites your flame.

Go as hard as you want as far as you can to
wherever your sites are aimed.
Cause and effect; result and foundation
Differentiates joy from happiness without
adding external stimuli to the equation.
Having what you want and wanting what you
have.
Are critical elements to prioritize and continue
down the path.
Reach for liberty.
Along with peace.
Be deliberate about putting your mind at ease.
Hesitate not to break away from harmful
bounds.
Peace of mind is more important; to yourself
make that vow.
Like a freshly discharged patient, or an inmate
newly released.
It's completely up to you to find the freedom
that you seek.

Check On You

Getting to know oneself is monumental knowledge worthy of the investment.
Weep for those who cannot stand to be alone.
Secluded moments equal a collection of thoughts that bring about the reality of why they're so lost.
Neglecting to conceive the notion that if they cannot stand to be with themselves how could anyone else.
Claiming faultless in the number of failed relationships and anyone who doesn't agree is a traitor.
But one moral look in the mirror will reveal the common denominator.
Seemingly immovable weights bearing down with the strength of lions.
Burdens meant to be carried by ten men, but this is a load only you can lighten.
Inflections in tone of voice render the sounds of attack.
Anytime someone comments on portrayed behavior not conducive to being on the right track.

Awaking often between the morning hours of 2
and 4 are good times for reflecting and to
rediscover.
It's a telltale sign that cortisol levels are high,
and adrenals need time to recover.
Being out of touch with your energy drags down
your temple eventually.
Throws off body chemistry and increases the
likelihood of dependency.
Losing the who you knew in you.
Further crippling yourself by refusing to take the
time to clear the only mind you have.
So many reference the term loyalty, but where is
that feature for yourself.
Show your soul a little love; stop putting it on
the shelf.
We all must play the hand that we were dealt.
There's nothing wrong with offering help.
Just know essence is no good if it remains
unhealed.
Check on you.

www.ingramcontent.com/pod-product-compliance
Lightning Source LLC
Chambersburg PA
CBHW051757130826
49812CB00033B/1187
9789357448161